C000283606

"Daddy's Working Away"

A Guide to
Being a Dad in Prison

Written by Inmates and Families at HMP Wolds
with Sandy Watson and Sheron Rice

Care for the Family

Designed by Allison Hodgkiss
Illustrated by Gerard Whyman

"Daddy's Working Away" Questionnaire

We hope you enjoyed the book! It would really help us to have your comments. If you could complete this short questionnaire and return it to the FREEPOST address overleaf, that would be great. Thanks!

- What did you think of the book? *(please circle)*

  Poor / **Fair** / **Good** / **Excellent**

- Was the book the right length? **Yes** / **No**
- Was the book easy to read? **Yes** / **No**
- Was the book helpful? **Yes** / **No**
- Which chapter or section of the book was the most helpful?

  Why?

- Was there a chapter or section of the book that was unhelpful? **Yes** / **No**

  If yes, what was it and why was it unhelpful?

- Were there any issues that you felt the book did not cover? **Yes** / **No**

  If yes, what would you like to have been included?

- Any other comments?

Name *(optional)*:

Are you *(please tick)*:

- A prisoner
- A tutor
- A prisoner's family member
- Other group/organisation

Name of prison/organisation:

Address:

Postcode:

Tel. No. *(if known)*:

Care for the Family - A Registered Charity.

Care for the Family
FREEPOST (CF4636)
Cardiff
CF15 7GZ

Contents

Foreword   v

Acknowledgements   vii

Introduction   ix

1   Going to Jail   1

2   The Big Question - What Do We Tell the Kids?   13

3   It's Good to Talk - Keeping in Contact   21

4   Wait 'til Your Father Gets Home! - Discipline   45

5   Money, Money, Money   53

6   Because You're Worth It! - You *and* Your Family   61

7   Tuning In - The Importance of Listening   71

8   School Issues - Helping Your Child Through   79

9   No Place Like Home - Preparing for Release   89

10   So Can You Really Be a Good Dad in Prison?   103

Group Discussion Questions   111

Social and Life Skills Tutors' Guide   117

Appendix - Useful Organisations   125

Foreword

A couple of years ago, Sandy Watson, the Parenting and Family Learning Co-ordinator at HMP Wolds, invited me to speak to some of the inmates attending her weekly classes.

As I stood before the men that day I can tell you that I felt totally inadequate for the task. What did I know about being a father while in prison? How could I enter into what they were feeling and the special pressures on their families? But they were looking to me for help, and they and their families had needs. I began:

'I know you don't choose to be in this institution - it is, in fact, the last place you want to be - but you *have* chosen to be with me for this session on parenting. And, therefore, you have done today what most fathers don't do in the whole of a lifetime - take time out to ask themselves the simple question, "How can I be a better father?"'

I went on to talk about a businessman I'd met who told me that he couldn't bring himself to hug his children. I told them I'd suggested to that man that he practise in front of a mirror! At the end of the session one of the prisoners approached me and said, 'At visiting times my family and I have to sit around a table. That table and the four chairs that surround it are screwed to the floor. One of the chairs is red and I have to sit on that chair. There are toys for the kids in the corner of the visiting room and sometimes my child will call to me to join her playing there, or perhaps she'll fall and need me. But I'm just not allowed off that chair. The prisoner then looked me straight in the eye and said, 'You tell the man who can't bring himself to hug his children about the man who can't get off the red chair.'

During 'question time' one of the men asked me if I would write a book that addressed the special needs of parents who are prisoners. Of course, I said that I couldn't, but then it struck me that perhaps we could help the men themselves to write such a book - who better to pass on lessons learned?

I count it a tremendous privilege to introduce this book to you. There is hardly a father on the face of the earth who doesn't have some regrets, who wouldn't welcome the chance to do things differently another time. I have no doubt that the men who compiled this book carry some of those regrets. Nevertheless, they are all determined, in spite of the enormous odds, to be the very best father they can be.

I believe that 'Daddy's Working Away' will be an enormous help to thousands of fathers in prison, but I also have a hunch that its lessons will go far beyond prison walls for, in truth, it reminds each of us what really matters as a dad.

I have written a couple of books myself - I know how hard it is - and I want to take this moment to offer the fathers of

HMP Wolds and their families my heartfelt congratulations. Books change people's lives and I have no doubt that this guide to being a dad in prison will do exactly that.

Rob Parsons
Executive Director,
Care for the Family

Acknowledgements

Our thanks go to the following organisations whose support has made this book possible:

Offenders' Learning and Skills Unit
Reading Families Millennium Awards Scheme
Mercers Charitable Foundation
Seedfield Trust
Swan Mountain Trust

Introduction

We're writing this book in the hope that it will help.

All of us here were dads one minute and prisoners the next and somehow the two things don't seem to fit together very well. Some of us felt we couldn't be a dad any more – just a prisoner.

When we talked about parenting in our education classes and had special family visits, we started to realise that there are things we can do to be a good dad and stay close to our kids.

We don't want to give the impression that we're sorted and everything is fine because that's just not true, but what we've realised is that there is hope - just a little - at the end of a very dark tunnel.

With our families, the inspiration and help of Sandy Watson our Parenting Tutor, and Sheron Rice of Care for the Family, we've put this book together. Hope you find it useful and encouraging.

Inmates at HMP Wolds

(All prisoners' and their families' names have been changed.)

Chapter 1
Going to Jail

MOVE DIRECTLY TO JAIL.

DO NOT PASS GO.

DO NOT COLLECT £200.

Sounds like a game. The reality is a nightmare.

Over one hundred thousand people a year are imprisoned and at any one time there are about seventy thousand people locked away in jail. The comforting part about this statistic is that most people only spend a short time inside, but however long it is, it is still precious time away from their families. Some families cope with it better than others.

Here are a few first-hand experiences ...

Mike - 6 years

It all happened so fast that day, no time to prepare, no chance to arrange a thing. There I was, for the first time in my life, arrested and locked up in a police cell. I didn't know what to expect so when I wasn't given any blankets and had the light on all night, I thought it must be normal.

I never did undress or get much sleep that night. I looked forward to the morning to be able to get a proper wash, but was disappointed to be led up the corridor to a tiny sink. No towel, no soap, no hot water and a custody officer who was definitely not interested in my well-being.

My breakfast consisted of a cup of tea and two filthy pieces of toast served by a man who hadn't seen a bath for years. Not only did I feel dirty, I felt alone and worried.

Lunch was not a lot better as it consisted of two
sandwiches and a cup of tea. I had another interview
that afternoon and was treated as Enemy of the State
Number One.

Evening came together with my dinner - beans and
sausage with a slice of bread and a cup of tea. I asked
if it was normal to have no blankets and the light on all
night and I was told that I should have asked. I was
handed some huge blankets and the light went out.
I didn't sleep any better though.

Sally

Every day I used to worry about my husband going to prison but he told me not to worry and he'd get mad if I told him my fears. So I kept my fears to myself and he shut himself off from me. He kept saying he wouldn't go to prison and I slowly began to believe what he was saying. They wouldn't send him to prison for an accident would they?

But it happened. He got two years.

I didn't want to go into court with him - I was too scared. When he didn't come out with his parents I was in a state of shock. I hadn't prepared myself for that. I hadn't had a chance to give him a proper goodbye. It hurt so much.

I couldn't believe what was happening. He'd said he would be coming out. I was scared; I didn't know what to do. I wondered how I would cope. What would I tell the children? They were waiting at home for their dad to come home, like he said he would.

I was worried about getting to see him. When would he get visitors? Would the children be able to visit him?

Would he cope in prison? Would it change him? Would he still want me? Our relationship wasn't at its best. I was scared of losing him forever.

I now know the answers, I know what to do now - wait for my husband because I love him. As for coping, I'm not doing a good job of that. I put on a brave face but inside I feel like crying all the time. I hold back the tears as I'm doing the shopping. Sometimes it's so hard, especially when the children want their dad or won't do as they're told. I feel like giving up but the children need me.

They know why their dad is away, I told them the day after. They still used to wait every day for him to come home, but now they think that he's never coming home. They're too young to understand, they think he doesn't want them any more.

We get to see him every week but it's hard to plan the visits, sort out transport and find the money - but we manage. We've got to keep the family together. It's hard to leave him after the visits, it often upsets the children, and they think it's their fault that he doesn't come home.

I worry every day about our future. The prison sentence has put a lot of stress on our relationship. I feel so alone. People say it gets easier, but it doesn't. Every day is hard and it goes so slow. I just want my husband home so we can be a family again.

Jess

It was very frightening. I wasn't used to being alone. Thoughts like, 'What if he's being bullied?' 'What if he can't cope?' kept coming to me. It was very worrying. I felt like my best friend as well as my loved one, had been taken away from me and my children. It isn't just the inmate that is being punished, it's the whole family.

Abi

I felt complete and utter devastation and disbelief. Nothing so horrible had ever happened before. My heart sank and my eyes filled with tears. I was so confused as to how this could happen to us. It felt like a bereavement, only no one had died.

Sheila

It was difficult hugging him before he went into court and then seeing him for just a few minutes behind the glass.

Chloe

My five-year-old was the worst because he thought that I had made his dad go away, so I got all the blame. Both children stopped eating for a good few weeks.

Natalie, aged 16

When my father told me he might be going to prison, I had a million emotions run through my head. He was not only my daddy, he was my mate and has always been there to talk to and offer as much support as he could.

My sister was admitted to hospital with pneumonia and whilst she was in hospital we were told that my dad was imprisoned for six whole years. I felt this sudden feeling in my chest as a heavy weight pulling down. It was like no pain I had ever felt. They took my dad when I most needed him.

Before my dad went to court he asked me to promise to stop making myself sick and I have kept that promise.

My mind is in constant deep thought about the past and why bad things happen all the time. I have to be strong for my dad because I love him. All I do now is look forward to the day he walks free and we can be a family again, me, my dad and my sister.

Suzy, aged 12

When I found out that my dad had been sentenced to ten months the first thing I did was work out whether he would be home for Christmas. I thought at least when he gets out he will be clean and I will see him more.

Joe - 14 years

When I was sentenced to fourteen years in 1993 I thought my life had come to an end. I had four children, one of them was two weeks old. What was going to happen?

Nazim - 12 months

At first I didn't know what to expect of prison except what I'd seen on telly. Cell Block H and Porridge came to mind, but most of all, leaving my wife and new-born son behind to cope on their own.

Dave - 6 years

For the first few days in prison there's a feeling of relief. Once this wears off you're left contemplating a long time away from your wife and children. This realisation, and the fact that the bottom line is it's your fault, leaves you with a heavy feeling of guilt. You know your family is going to suffer as well and they've done no wrong.

Do any of these stories sound familiar?

We realise that when someone goes to prison it causes immense heartache for all the members of the family. We've tried hard in this book to suggest a few ways of making the separation more bearable and to give a few practical tips that we dads have found helpful.

The next few chapters will look at what you can tell the kids about being in prison and will make some suggestions about phone-calls, letters and making the most of visits. We'll look at how you get involved in discipline and how to handle money problems. We'll also tackle issues such as listening to your children, making them feel good about themselves and how to help with their education. Finally we'll suggest ways to prepare you and your family for freedom.

It's our firm belief that we can be good dads, even though we're in prison. We really hope the book will help you come to believe that for yourself, too. All the best!

For personal study

- What was your reaction when you were sentenced?

- What were your partner's and children's reactions?

- Have you been able to talk to your partner and children about this?

- What are the main difficulties your family has to face due to you being in prison?

- What are your needs as a parent, now you are in prison?

- Is there any way those needs can be met?

- Write your own experience of 'Going to jail'.

Chapter 2
The Big Question -
What Do We Tell the Kids?

We thought this was going to be an easy chapter to write. Our ideas started off with things like, 'Honesty is the best policy' and, 'Tell the truth, the whole truth and nothing but the truth …' Comments flew around like, 'You've got to tell them the truth, you're their dad!' or, 'What if a relative, or someone at school, lets the cat out of the bag? Isn't it better that you're the one to tell them?'

But a few of us started to shift uncomfortably in our chairs when we went round each person to ask what *he* had told his children. Bravely someone announced, 'All this talk of honesty is fine, but my little 'un thinks I'm working away.' Then someone else chipped in, 'My little lad's only four so he doesn't really understand what prison is. So basically, he doesn't know I'm here either.'

Deafening silence around the table. Where do we go from here?

In the end we felt that we would try and cover all sides, looking at all the pros and cons (no pun intended) of telling your kids that you are in jail.

Here are some of the things we think are worth considering.

🤔 Your child's age

Your child's age will obviously come into the reckoning. A young child or toddler probably isn't going to be aware of the issue of prison, so perhaps doesn't need to be told about it. But what about the child who is, let's say, at junior school and probably understands a little about prison from bits picked up on the news or television. Maybe he'll start to wonder about that big building he visits regularly to see you, or why you don't even come home for holidays when the

few other dads who work away do seem to come home from time to time.

As children approach their teenage years, they are highly unlikely to accept the 'Dad's working away' version of events, and it's only right and proper that you treat them like young adults and give them as much of the truth as you are able. If you are in for a very serious crime, then you may not want to say anything about the offence itself; bear in mind though, that in view of the fact that you will no doubt be mentioned in all the local newspapers, you may *need* to tell them about it.

So when is the best time to tell them? Well … there isn't a definite answer! Every child is different and every family situation is different. You must use your intuition since, as their parents, no one knows your child better than you do. You must decide when it's best.

The length of your sentence

The length of your sentence will also count when it comes to telling your child that you are in jail. For example, a twelve-month sentence will mean, in effect, the prisoner serving half that time and maybe being eligible for tagging after four months. If that's you, you may feel able to justify your being away for four months - only you know that though.

For medium length sentences of, say, three to four years, the prisoner could reasonably expect to go to a Category D open prison quite quickly and, after assessment, he would get weekly town visits. If this is your situation it would mean that you could see your children regularly, and if they are young this might stop them asking as many questions.

With long sentences the problems mount. Visits will be in restricted surroundings and children will quickly ask why you can't come home with them. One way of dealing with young children here is to begin to give them information gradually by saying that, 'Daddy's been naughty and can't go out.' The child will equate this with being kept in or sent to bed. The problem comes when they start to discuss this outside the family circle.

😕 If you don't tell them, someone else will

If your case had a lot of publicity, or if the locals all know about it, there's a good chance your child will get to hear about it too. Other children may hear their parents or others talking and 'put two and two together'. Children can be cruel to one another, we all know that, and all of a sudden they've got a perfect target to tease next playtime … your little one! And if your child is teased about you being in jail, it can cause all sorts of trauma. If you are upfront about being in prison, hopefully, at least, your child can come and talk this through with you and not suffer in silence.

Whether your family has had to move home

If, for financial or social reasons, your family had to move house after you went to prison, your children may have had to change school and leave friends behind. It may be a lot fairer in this situation to explain to them why this has all come about.

Stuart - 2 years

I haven't told my children that I'm in prison. Even my eldest (aged six) thinks I'm at work. I think telling them would affect them even more. I don't want to upset them, and as long as they know that I love them, I don't think it matters.

Paul - 6 years

I've told them I'm at work because that's all they can understand (they're one and two years old). When they're older, I'll be honest with them and say I made a mistake.

Sean - 6 months

I've told him that I'm working away. I'll be home before
long, so he'll never need to know.

Paddy - 3 years

We've told her the truth. She's old enough to understand
the consequences of drugs.

Vince - 2 years

We've told her that I'm in prison for being naughty. We
thought it best to tell the truth before someone else told her.

OK, so what <u>should</u> you tell your kids?

Several of us decided initially that we'd want to be absolutely 'up front' with our kids about what has happened to us so that we could 'get things off our chests'. It was only when we stopped to think about the implications of doing this that we realised it may be a selfish gesture in some cases. Others of us argued that we were, in fact, being more responsible parents by shielding our child from the harsh realities of our situation.

There really is no right and wrong answer to this question, but it does need to be something that you and your partner work out together.

Things can be even more difficult if you would prefer to tell your children the truth, but your partner has already told them that you are working away. If this happens you would have to decide together whether it would be less confusing and upsetting for the children to continue to believe her version of events, or whether your reasons for telling them the truth are more important.

It's a tough decision to make isn't it? - although we hope that weighing up some of the things we've discussed will help you come to a decision. As you can see, we're sitting firmly on the fence about it! But, whatever decision you come to, our thoughts are with you and your families.

For personal study

- What have you told your children about your sentence?

- Why did you tell them this?

- Write two lists, one showing the advantages of telling your child the truth, and another showing the disadvantages of telling the truth.

- An inmate comes to you for advice on 'the big question'. What would you suggest to him if his children were aged three and eleven?

Chapter 3
It's Good to Talk - Keeping in Contact

It's a great temptation in prison to cut all family ties and do our time 'hard-core': no contact - no phone calls, visits or letters - just waiting and seeing what the situation is when we finally get out. Many of us do just that. But keeping in contact is crucial to being a good dad in prison - and that's why this chapter has turned out to be the longest!

Just in case you're not convinced, think about this: if your child is ten years old now, 3650 days of his childhood have already gone. You have 2920 left until they are 18! Do you want to miss being out of touch for even one of those days if you can help it?

Frank - 15 years

Yes, I've been tempted to cut all ties. It would stop a lot of upset and worry. It seems an easy option - out of sight out of mind - but this would only confuse the kids and it would put all the strain on their mother. Easier for me though.

Jed - 2 years

Yes, I've cut all ties. We (me and my ex) kept falling out; there were too many problems. It's easier to let go while you are in prison.

Sam - 4 years

Never! When I first got my sentence, me and my partner had a talk to each other and said that no matter what happens we are both here for each other - for better and for worse.

Pierre - 14 years

I decided that on my first visit I would tell my wife that we should call it a day. My wife was young, she should start again with someone new. I wanted to give her the chance, but what I wanted to hear was that she would wait for me. When they (my wife and four children) came up on the visit and I told them what I had been thinking, they all started to cry and blamed me for not loving them. Anyway, we all stood by each other and, after seven years, we are a lot stronger for it. Don't get me wrong, we've had some horrible times, and there have been times when I've thought that we couldn't take any more, but I've got through them knowing there are better times to come.

There are three ways of keeping in contact from prison - by phone, mail or visits. Let's start with the phone.

The phone

'ET, phone home!' became a bit of a catch phrase a few years ago but the difficulty that ET had in keeping contact with home is nothing compared with what we inmates have to put up with!

Just think about it. As long as he went in disguise, ET could go anywhere and had extra powers to help him keep in touch. An inmate, however, has limited access to a phone, and often the only time is early evening when it's bedtime/teatime - and probably when the Simpsons is on! Unlike an inmate, ET did not have restrictions on the number of phone-cards he could have in his possession. ET also never had to suffer the disheartening situation of listening to his own voice on an answering machine because his other half was busy upstairs putting the kids to bed!

The phone can be a great way of keeping in touch with your loved ones, but it is not without its frustrations and difficulties.

Bill - 2 years

I keep in contact with my children every night. I spend about £1 a night on the phone and send about ten letters home a week.

Chris - 6 months

I spend every penny of my wages on keeping in contact with my family. I'd rather go without things than not keep up with what's going on at home.

Jay - 3 months

It's a big decision sometimes. Do I phone home or get some baccy? It's really hard for those of us who smoke.

Mal - 10 years

As much as I am desperate to talk to them, I realise that their routine has been disrupted enough through my absence, so if I can't get through to them at the right time, I leave it. I'm not the one who has to get them up in the morning if they've stayed up late talking to Dad!

Phil - 2 years

I've stopped phoning home as all me and my partner do is row all the time.

Ian - 5 years

I hate it when I phone home and there's no answer. I start to worry as to what has happened to them. I imagine all kinds of unimagineables.

Fred - 9 months

It's important to plan your phone-calls. A bad phone-call can ruin your day. I know lots of men who have 'kicked off' big style after a row on the phone.

Paul - 12 years

I phone the kids up and wish them, 'Happy Christmas', but then I've got four kids on the phone crying and I've just spoiled it for them. What am I supposed to do?

Mary

I make every effort to keep in as much contact with Gerry as possible. The telephone has helped us a lot. His voice is a great thing to hear, it's a life-saver. It eases a lot of pain to speak to him, but when we finish on the phone I'm left with such emptiness.

Jan

Every time the phone rings she runs to it and says,
'Hello daddy, I love you' - it doesn't matter who it is!
It makes her day to talk to him on the phone.

Sarah

I never get to talk to him these days, the kids use up all of
his credits telling him every little detail of the day - what
they had for tea and what they did at school. It's worth it
though, they love to talk to their dad.

Letters

Because of the emotion involved in a phone-call, some inmates tend to stick with writing letters. It's also easier sometimes to pour out your true thoughts and feelings on paper.

Kids love getting a letter especially when it's addressed personally to them and no one else. Although it's nice to be able to buy your kids things when you've got the money, having a letter through the post can make their day.

Alan - 3 years

My daughter keeps all my letters to her under her pillow and reads them before she goes to sleep.

Neil - 2 years

It costs me a fortune! Each of my kids wants a letter each at least once a week. I get into trouble if I send one to the Missus and not to them!

Karen (to husband, Paul)

Jimmy (aged three) was well pleased when he got a letter off you. He got really excited and listened to me so I could read it. He kept saying it was HIS letter and not mine. As I was reading it to him, he put his head on my shoulder and you could see him smiling and dreaming. It was like he could see you talking to him.

'Dear Johns' - so how do you keep in contact now?

There are some letters that are very traumatic to read and can leave us devastated for a long time. Letters known as 'Dear Johns' - where your partner tells you she's leaving you - are particularly bad news.

And a 'Dear John' letter when you've got kids is not only bad, but complicated.

OK, so you and your partner weren't exactly getting on and therefore it's no surprise that she's found someone else, but your first thoughts are: 'What will happen to the kids?' 'Will she still bring them to see me?' and 'Will they start to think this new bloke is their dad?'

The problem is even more complicated if the children are not your 'real' kids, but you've taken them on board as your own, have been with them for several years and they've only ever known you as their dad. Now what? Your partner definitely doesn't want to see you again. What rights have you got?

Maybe you're one of the lucky ones and you and your partner are still 'friends', so that she's happy to bring the kids on visits to spend time with you. Maybe you're not so lucky and the two of you can't manage to speak two words together without World War Three breaking out. Maybe your kids will be used as pawns; stuck in the middle of no-man's land, confused and bitter.

Phil - 7 years

I felt scared that I was going to lose the kids. Was this bloke going to want them to call him 'Dad'? Was he going to try and take my family away from me?

Mark - 4 months

I felt a feeling of anger and betrayal. She only had to wait a few months for me!

Seventy percent of men get 'Dear Johns'. If I get one, I get one. You can't expect the woman to wait around for eight years!

Mandy (to Rod)

I love you, babe, and this is the last thing I want to do to you, especially when you're in there, but I've taken all I can take and I'm calling it a day.

If you've had a 'Dear John', unfortunately there's no magic solution to your predicament - but we do have just a few suggestions from lads who have been there:

✓ Try to have a good relationship and be as pleasant as you can to your partner since she's the one who is looking after your children. Abuse and threats may cause her to take legal action against you.

✓ Try and enlist the help of grandparents, relatives or friends to bring the children on visits.

✓ Don't use the kids as pawns. Always speak well of your partner to your children. Don't make them choose between you and her.

✓ Keep up with writing letters to the kids. Get photocopies made if you think your letters aren't getting through.

✓ If your efforts to communicate fail, involve a solicitor.

✓ Contact other organisations for support and advice (see appendix).

Visits

A visit with your children will go much better if you plan it a bit beforehand rather than just turning up and seeing what happens. It may involve you writing down a list of questions to ask them or even a couple of jokes to tell. Sounds crazy doesn't it? But the fact is that these visits will go more smoothly if you are prepared.

Try and anticipate the kind of journey your family will have had. How will your partner be feeling if she's had to drive a long way with three travel-sick or squabbling children in the back? Does your teenager suffer with mood swings, and, if so, how will you jolly her out of it? What will you do if your child won't talk to you on the visit? What if your partner wants you to take an active role in disciplining and keeps urging you to 'Tell him off' or 'Give her what for'?

Pete and his family suffered a series of difficult visits that involved lots of 'telling-offs' and 'sorting-outs' - and, not surprisingly, resulted in some very discouraging times. Billy, a Listener, suggested that they stopped using visits as 'sorting-out' times and concentrated on making them an enjoyable experience for everyone. When Pete's family discussed this they decided that is what they would do, leaving 'sorting-out' to letters and phone-calls. Nowadays they all look forward to visits rather than dreading them!

Facilities for children vary from prison to prison. At best they can offer a designated play area with play-workers, extended family visits, Christmas parties, family meals and brunch. In some cases, a Family Learning Programme is run where a prisoner and his partner can attend a weekly playgroup with their children. A certificate is awarded at the end of the course.

At worst, some prisons offer very few facilities - perhaps just a box of toys in a corner of the visiting room. You can find out what facilities a prison has by consulting the Prisoner's Handbook - and maybe it's a good idea to find what a prison offers before requesting a transfer.

Stevie - 6 years

Visits are like a roller-coaster ride of emotions with very high points and very low points - full of contradictions. For example, it's great to see each other, but it breaks your heart to part at the end. It's also great to see the children, but they put so much pressure on their mum, making her anxious. Sometimes I want to stop all my visits, but I can't.

Jason - 8 months

When my little ones come to visit me they throw off their shoes and run for the play area, which is great for them. When they finally come to the table for a drink I try and read a book to them, but they just want to go off and play. They can't understand that I'm stuck on this red seat.

Tim - 4 years

I spend the whole of the visit waving at my little girl on the climbing frame. I'm glad she enjoys her visit, but sometimes I feel like a spare part.

Rob - 4 years

Visits are great! I get the kids to bring in their school books and I always manage to hear them read and we have a good laugh together. The play area is great as they can always go there when they get bored and it means me and my girlfriend get time to chat too.

Samantha
(Greig's wife, writing about the Christmas Party)

Thank you for providing the entertainment on the visit, it really did make a huge difference. Greig and our daughter, Rachel, have a brilliant relationship and can talk very easily to each other, but on a normal visit that is the only thing they can do. Them being able to play together, instead of just facing each other across a table, made for a good change.

Margo

It was hard to accept that he didn't want the kids to visit him - until I'd seen what it was like. Now I know why!

So … keeping in contact. Is it worth the hassle?

Let's face it, if you shut your family out and forget about them until you are released, you could possibly cope better because you wouldn't have any of those emotional roller-coaster feelings. But this book is about being a *dad* in prison and like all dads we have to make sacrifices and do things that don't suit us, but are good for the kids. We have to make choices that are not for our benefit - you know the kind I mean on the out: 'Do I go to the football match with my mates or watch "Monster's Inc." at the cinema with three little girls?' It's a tough one!

It is difficult to keep in contact with your loved ones when you are in prison. It requires money for stamps and phone-calls, it requires patience in waiting for your turn on the phone, and it requires determination to stick at it, even when you know that sometimes your letters don't get through to your kids or are read by third parties. It

sometimes means coming back from a visit that has gone so badly wrong that you feel you can't cope anymore and are depressed and angry. It means riding on that emotional roller-coaster. It is not without personal cost.

But what does making an effort to keep in contact say to our children? It tells them that we love them and are thinking about them throughout the week. It tells them we would love to be with them and that we miss them. It tells them that even though we've made mistakes and have ended up in prison, we are still their dad - and nothing is going to stop us from being there for them.

What would we do? Well, personally, we really enjoyed 'Monster's Inc.'!!!!

Things you can do

✓ A letter addressed to a specific child can make his or her day. A special telephone call on birthdays, exam dates, sports days, and so on, can help children to feel loved and cared for. Don't let your child think that for one moment you've lost interest in them. Make a note of special events and days on your calendar to help you remember.

✓ In your pad, make a card for your child with a few felt tip pens - it shows that you've thought about her. It will kill time and mark you out as a family man. Remember that a stable family background is a big factor in getting parole in some cases - not that you should maintain contact for this reason.

✓ Don't be frightened to give your children a hug or a kiss on visits. They may be embarrassed and say something like, 'Stop it, Dad, everyone's watching,' but they'll know you care. It's amazing how many dads don't say a simple, 'love you' to their kids every now and again.

Daddy or toys?
- a child's view of a visit

When we got out of the car, my mum spat on her hanky and wiped my face 'cos she said it was dirty.

We went into a big room and there were lots of pictures on the walls. There was a lady selling sweets and ice-cream, but I couldn't have one 'cos my mum says all her money has to go to my dad.

We went to a big man behind a desk. He looked like a policeman without a hat on, but he smiled and said hello to me. Mum gave him some bits of paper - I wanted to carry them, but she said they were really special and if I lost them I couldn't see my dad - so I let her carry them.

We went to sit down, but Mum wanted a cig so we had to go outside. I wanted the toilet so Mum put her cig out and we went back inside. Then there was a loud voice coming out of a little box on the wall and my mum said it was our turn.

We went outside again and across a road to some big doors. There was another policeman who wanted to look at our bits of paper as well.

Then I had to put my coat and bag on a big machine, like that one at school where Miss copies things, and we walked through a doorway with no door. It made a funny noise and Mum had to give the Mister our car keys. I hoped he wouldn't pinch it!

I was frightened when the man had a big gun with a long light on - but he said it wasn't a gun, it was a magic wand for finding pennies and metal things. Then he gave me a special bracelet like Mum's, and he put something on my hand - but I don't think it worked 'cos I couldn't see it. I had to give a lady and another Mister my coat and bag and they put them in a metal box with Mum's handbag.

Then we went through some more doors. They were funny because they had to close before the next ones would open. Another walk and my legs were getting tired, but the lady with us said it wasn't far.

A Mister looked at my bracelet and my hand - I was going to tell him there was nothing there but my mum said ssssshhhhh!

Then I saw a little brown and white dog. It was sitting down near some people in front of us and lots of Misters were telling them they couldn't go in - I think.

My mum was still carrying the special paper when we went into another room, but then she gave them to one of the Misters behind the desk. He looked funny 'cos I think he had a Walkman on just like Daddy's.

I wanted to go and play but I had to wait until Daddy came in. I gave him a hug and a kiss. Then he started kissing Mummy, it lasted for ages.

I wanted to play with the big orange tractor, but a little boy was on it first. My daddy once told me what to do if someone had what you wanted - I think that's why he is here.

I had to stay with Mummy and Daddy 'cos she said, 'Which did I want, Daddy or toys?' and I love my dad, even more than a big tractor (I think).

# For personal study

- How regularly do you keep in contact with your family?

- Is your family happy with the amount of contact they have?

- What works best for you - visits, phone-calls or letters? Why?

- Think about a typical visit from your family (if you get any).
    What could you do to improve these visits?
    What could the prison do to help improve these visits?

- Read "Daddy or toys?", how one prisoner saw a visit through his child's eyes. Imagine you are your child and try to write your version of the visit from his or her point of view.

Chapter 4
Wait 'til Your Father Gets Home! - Discipline

The issue of how we maintain discipline is one that provokes a lot of reaction and frustration. All of us dads see discipline as part of our role, but we admit that we feel powerless to do anything to maintain it while we're in prison.

There are often arguments and conflict with our partner over badly behaving kids and how to deal with them. Phone-calls are often stressful - particularly when our partner puts our child on the phone saying, 'You sort him out!' Although the child may well *need* sorting-out, we feel that we have so little quality time with them that any contact we do have should be positive and fun, not a whole load of 'telling-offs. As a result discipline is usually left to Mum.

In fact, in society as a whole, this is generally the case. Since fathers are often out at work - perhaps even working away! - it's usually the mother who is left at home to look after young children and therefore it's natural for her to deal them out when they misbehave. When she's had a bad day with the kids, a mum's last resort may well be in the form of, 'Wait 'til your father gets home'. Knowing that she is able to make this threat may give her that little bit of breathing space she needs - especially when she's at her wit's end. What she needs most is the support and backing of her partner.

You may feel frustrated that you cannot be more directly involved and angry when your partner uses you as a threat to the kids, but being frustrated about it won't help her. What she needs to know is that you are behind her one hundred percent.

'What can I do, luv?"

Perhaps a good way of starting would be to ask your partner *how* you can support her. Tell her that you don't want to always be seen as the bad guy, but also be willing to 'have words' with the children when she asks you to. Encourage her by telling her how well she is doing and saying that she has your full support.

It's crucial that you discuss discipline issues together and if you have major disagreements about how to go about things, you need to come to some kind of compromise. Don't be too critical of your partner - 'You're too soft/hard with him' - as this will put her on the defensive. Remember that, as with everything else in life, it's always easier said than done.

Continue to back your partner in front of the children, even if you don't agree with what she is doing. Saying things to your children like, 'Well, if I were home, *I'd* let you ...' will unsettle the child and cause them to play one of you off against the other.

Of course, you may well be in a situation where your partner refuses to discuss these things with you and excludes you from knowing what is really going on. This is painfully frustrating for you but not a lot can be done. Even if this is happening to you, it's still important to support your partner and, by doing so, you may well eventually win her trust.

So now you're an expert?

Many dads in prison do parenting courses and get some good ideas on how to sort out minor discipline issues. However, passing these ideas on to your partner can go down like a lead balloon! Giving her the benefit of your wisdom when she's just telling you about a bad incident with your screaming child in the supermarket is probably not helpful for her!

Perhaps a good idea would be to write and tell her about the kinds of things you've been learning. Suggest she buys (or borrows from the library) one of the course books you found helpful. If you can do this when things are *not* at crisis point, you may find that she is more willing to listen to your ideas. Perhaps on the next visit you can put some of your theories into practice and show her how it's done!

Don't give up!

Garry - 10 months

I'll phone and tell them off if I hear they're doing wrong.

Mike - 3 months

I leave it to her, 'cos I'm not there.

Tommy - 3 years

They live with her, so I don't have much contact. They probably wouldn't listen anyway.

Boz - 7 years

I ring up and give them what for if she asks me to. They say, 'Sorry, Dad' and all that but you know that once you put the phone down they're laughing their heads off and you can't do a thing about it.

Ginger - 12 months

She'll bring them on a visit and ask me to have a word with them, but I try and advise rather than chastise.

Bruce - 6 months

It's hard, but I do what I can to help her out with discipline. It's no fun for her having to sort it out on her own.

Dai - 2 years

I feel totally powerless.

Top tips on discipline

✓ Be loving and supportive

Discipline that is done in a loving and positive environment - that is, complimenting our children when they do well, showing love and affection for them, listening to and understanding them - *will work.*

Children who are constantly criticised, laughed at and not given any attention will not respond well. Research has shown that for every negative thing we say to our child we have to balance it with four positives for it to become effective. That's not a bad thing to remember when we hear ourselves nagging at our children.

✓ Be realistic!

Try to find out a bit about child development and what we can reasonably expect of our children. It would be crazy to expect our three-year-old to have got the dinner ready or keep her room spotlessly tidy. Maybe, however, we would expect our teenager to help prepare a meal occasionally.

Likewise, it's unrealistic to expect young children to sit quietly on a visit. By nature they are inquisitive and perhaps want to wander round the visiting hall, getting into places they shouldn't. We're not, for one minute, suggesting we leave them to get up to mischief, but we are saying it's not realistic to expect one hundred percent good behaviour. Perhaps by giving them a little more attention, reading a book, or telling them a story, they may remain attentive for a little longer, but if there are no play workers or facilities for children, then it might be better to organise a short visit, or bring the grandparents along so they can take the children out when they begin to get bored.

✓ Be clear and consistent (and remember that discipline has got to make sense)

It's important that you give clear and consistent rules to your children, explaining why they can or can't do things:

- 'I want you to come home at tea time because it's not safe for you to play outside when it's dark.'
- 'You mustn't touch the oven when it's on, because it's hot and will burn you.'
- 'You can't play football near those houses because you might break a neighbour's window, but you can go to the park after tea and play then.'

So dads, do we take, 'Wait 'til your father gets home,' literally and wash our hands of any part in disciplining our kids until we leave prison, or can we do something now?

As usual, we can't give you a definite answer. Situations will vary from family to family and how much of a role you can take will depend on the ages of the children and their temperament. But let's leave you with this thought: when we looked up the word 'discipline' in a dictionary we saw that its main definition is 'training'.

Can we possibly leave our children's 'training' to one person or, indeed, until we get out of prison? Isn't it best for our kids to get trained by as many good influences as possible, even though some of their 'trainers' may not be on hand as much as others?

 ## For personal study

- Do you think that you are able to discipline your child while you are in prison?

- What does your partner think?

- What would you do if your four-year-old kept getting into trouble on a visit?

- What would you do if your partner put your nine-year-old on the phone and told you to give her a good telling off?

- Write down one thing that you would like to change in your child's behaviour.

- Write down four things you like about your child - then write a letter and tell them!

Chapter 5
Money, Money, Money

The issue of money and financial support for your family is a difficult one for everybody.

If you were used to being the family's 'Breadwinner' you may find it especially difficult because you have to struggle with the fact that the family you used to provide for now have to survive on benefits. You may feel guilty that they've lost their old standard of living and, on prison wages of around £7.50 a week, you are powerless to do anything to help. On the other hand, if your family was on benefits before your imprisonment, then they probably won't notice much of a change in their finances and maybe you won't feel the guilt quite so keenly.

Dealing with debt

If you arrive in prison up to your neck in debt it's important to deal with the situation in the best way possible. You can contact the Citizen's Advice Bureau for help and some prisons have Welfare or Throughcare systems that can support you.

If someone owes you money and doesn't pay it back or get in contact with you, what happens? You get angry! But if

they get in touch and give you a reason why they can't pay,
although you might still be annoyed, at least you know
what's happening and can plan accordingly.

Businesses work in exactly the same way and so it's far better
to contact those to whom you owe money, explain your
situation and try to agree a way of sorting it out. If you have
a mortgage, for example, and have never been in arrears
before, a building society will often waive repayments for up
to two years or more if they are kept informed about what is
happening. Finance companies and the like can be far more
flexible than many of us imagine.

And if any creditors are pressing your family too hard, they
are committing a criminal offence and could finish up in the
cell next door to you!

Helping your family financially

Can you give financial support to your family when you are in prison? The answer is probably a resounding NO. In fact, you are more likely to be a burden to them by asking for new trainers, underwear etc.

However, you can be a help to your family by taking a keen interest in the finances and asking if they are getting all the benefits to which they are entitled. If there are difficult forms to complete, ask your partner to send them to you and see if you can make sense of them. If you can't understand the forms, another inmate or member of staff may be able to help. Talk to the kids about having to cut back - 'Sorry, we would love to be able to get you that bike, but we can't just yet'. Children show remarkable understanding when things are explained to them and they are consulted.

Some partners, we know, will not want to share the extent of their financial crisis with you for fear of worrying you. In these situations you just have to be patient and continue to reassure your partner without badgering her.

Towards the end of longer sentences there are facilities for working out of jail on licence. These jails help inmates to find jobs, so that for the last part of their sentence they can earn and save money that can be sent to the family. Being able to do this also means that you can be self-sufficient, not having to rely on outside help for money.

The role of supporting the family financially *is* difficult to carry out in prison, but remember that it's also difficult being unable to earn through unemployment or illness. Giving your partner emotional support, and showing that you want to help, can go some way to fulfilling this role.

Karen, partner of Roland

He worries about money too much. We survive - not brilliantly but we do. It was money troubles that got him in to trouble in the first place!

Visiting expenses

The APVU (Assisted Prison Visits Unit) helps towards the cost of a visit every fourteen days, although the actual day of visiting can vary. To qualify for this you must meet the income criteria and will need to apply direct to the APVU (see appendix). Additional help may be available if visitors need to stay overnight or need someone to travel with them because of a medical condition. Expenses can be provided in advance of the visit or after and the visitor should make sure she has a "Confirmation of a Visit" form date stamped at the prison when she visits.

John - 8 months

I transferred everything I own into my partner's name and made a will, but I still worry.

Barney - 14 months

If it wasn't for the APVU and my family, my wife would not be able to visit. She's just surviving really.

Ahmed - 10 years

Financially my wife should be OK but I'm concerned that what I'm in for, and the further investigations, may affect her home and business.

Bob - 5 months

My family is looking after me because I was arrested on the street and had only thirty pence in my pocket.

Gary - 12 years

We didn't realise I would be getting such a long sentence so we never planned long term. All the savings we had are now gone. It's surprising how much you do need when you have two young children. It's a big worry for me.

Richard - 12 months

Even though I need a couple of things I'm reluctant to ask for money to be sent in as I don't want to put additional pressures on my partner.

What to do if you have financial worries:

✓ Ask for professional help as soon as you arrive in prison.

✓ Check whether you have any benefit entitlement - the Citizens Advice Bureau and Welfare or Throughcare will help you find out.

✓ Keep your family informed of your situation.

✓ Do a "Budgeting and Money Management" course.

✓ Save as much as you can - even a small amount can make a difference.

For personal study

- Which best describes your financial situation?

  - "My family is well provided for"
  - "My family is struggling"
  - "My kids have got everything they need"
  - "I'm worried about my debts"

- Have you ever considered applying for debt counselling?

- Is your family claiming all the benefits they are entitled to?

- Apply to do a "Budget and Money Management" course.

Chapter 6
Because You're Worth It! -
You *and* Your Family

An important job for parents is to help their children grow up confident and happy, and our aim in this chapter is to talk about how we can build up our kids' self-esteem. But before we can do that, we need to think carefully about our opinion of ourselves. If our self-esteem is very low, it will be really difficult to help someone else.

Feeling a failure

It won't be a surprise to you that many prisoners have a very poor opinion of themselves.

> *The judge sentences you to years and you are led out of court to the sound of crying from your newly pregnant partner, the look of horror on your mum's face, and your three kids screaming and shouting 'Daddy'. Your partner warned you not to get involved, but you were concerned about paying the mortgage. Your dad offered you all his savings to pay off your debt, but you were too proud to accept his help. You told your family that you would sort it. Now you've landed them all in it, big time.*

It's hard to feel good about yourself in such a situation. The feelings of failure and being worthless come far more easily.

On top of that you lose your name and identity and become just a number, a part of the system. It's easy to slip into depression and feel there's no point in anything any more ... it's too late.

Most of us, then, have some pretty negative feelings when we're first sentenced but the key thing is not to let them get to you.

Talking about it

The first thing to do is to talk to someone - a problem shared is a problem halved and all that. Maybe you can't talk to your pad mate - especially if he's not the sensitive type! - so ask the officers to put you in contact with the Listeners.

The Listeners are a branch of the Samaritans and are a group of inmates trained to give support. They aren't paid for this work, nor do they earn Brownie points for doing it. They are often called out at all hours to talk to people and there's always someone available on call. They're not a bunch of do-gooders, just guys who want to give back a little of the support they were given themselves when they were new. They will introduce you to others on the Unit and fill you in on the system. But the most important thing is that everything you say is totally CONFIDENTIAL.

You should also consider a visit to Healthcare who may be able to help and support you. And should you feel that, even with this support, you still can't cope, you can ask to see one of the trained counsellors - though this may take some time, depending on their availability.

The Chaplaincy team are also always available to talk with you and they run a variety of groups that may help you with your difficulties.

The end of the line ...

If you are really depressed and considering your 'options', (suicide or self harm), there *is* help - but you must tell someone straight away how you are feeling. Your loved ones can also voice their concerns about you through a confidential help line.

Once the officers are made aware of how you are feeling, you may find what happens next surprising. There's no laughing at you or poking fun. You will be put on a suicide or self-harm 'watch' and your routine will be recorded at regular intervals in an orange booklet. The cell night-light is left on, the door flap left open, and a regular check made of your welfare day and night.

These are some comments from people who have been on a 'watch':

"No-one took the mick, everyone seemed to actually care".

"It's weird at first - but then you realise that someone's really listening to you".

"I got a chance to say things I wouldn't normally say, and people listened".

These 'watches' are reviewed on a weekly basis and everyone involved in them will speak to you and find out how you really feel. Everything you say will be kept confidential and nothing is discussed with people who don't need to know. No-one penalises you for being depressed, but they can only help if you let them.

"I was on a watch after attempting suicide shortly after being sentenced. Everyone's been a big help, and I'm now at a stage where things don't seem so bad and I can now ask for help when I need it. No-one will turn away if they can help and if they can't, they'll find someone who can".

One piece of advice:

"You get the chance to tell the truth about how you *really* feel - take it!"

Education

One way to increase your self-esteem in prison is to improve your skills by joining an education course. Perhaps you can't read or write very well? - Well, this is a good time to learn. Scared stiff of computers? - Get on an IT course and tell your kids all about it. Let them know that when you get out, you're going to want some time on their PC! Design a certificate on the computer and send it to your child for doing well at school/home. That will be a boost for him as well as you!

Think about taking some qualifications, especially if you're good at certain subjects. Some men end up doing GCSEs at the same time as their kids, so there's a bit of competition to see who gets the highest grade. (You can also check up on how much revision they are doing!)

Adrian - 10 years

Getting a GCSE is the best thing that ever happened to me. I'm 60 and have never done an exam in my life. I can't tell you how it feels to succeed at something at my age.

Justin - 6 years

I would never have believed I could do exams. All of my life I'd been told I was stupid. I wish those people could see me now!

Join an Arts and Crafts course and make some things to send home. If you are really good at this, you may be able to exhibit and sell some of your work at prison exhibitions. The annual Koestler awards show the kind of talent that can be found in prison.

Health and exercise

Get to the gym. Find that six-pack you used to have and impress the missus! Go to one of the well-man sessions which looks at diet, health and fitness. Use this time to go on drugs, alcohol courses or whatever your poison was, and kick the habit once and for all!

Through doing these kinds of things you'll start to feel better about yourself and this will have a knock-on effect on your partner and kids. They'll respect your efforts and feel better about their own worth as a family.

Encouraging your family

Once you are feeling more positive about yourself you'll then be able to encourage and build up your family. Praise your partner for doing well with the kids; tell her she looks nice and thank her for holding things together. Make sure you say something positive to each of the children. Tell them in letters that you are proud of them, point out all the good qualities they have and send them certificates when they've made extra special efforts.

It is possible, however, that when you start feeling better about yourself, your partner will go through a bad patch. While you were going under, she was holding everything together, she had to keep going, but now it may be her turn to feel low and lack confidence. Encourage her at this time. Perhaps suggest she gets out a bit more or treats herself. Try to arrange for grandparents to have the kids every now and then and, if the finances can cope, talk her into taking the kids on a holiday. Make sure she is getting all the benefits she is entitled to. Be strong for her.

Graham - 6 months

I go to the gym; it helps me feel good about myself. And the kids? Well I let them know that there is an end to all this. Daddy is coming home.

Amir - 12 years

My family keep me going; I send letters all the time to the kids. I always let them know that I love them no matter what.

Daryl - 8 years

My son is mad on football and had scored two goals at the last match. When I was in the IT lesson I printed him a certificate for his achievement. You should have seen his face when he saw it. He was over the moon with it! It's now in pride of place on his bedroom wall.

Karl - 4 years

I'm waiting till I get out; there's not a lot you can do whilst you are in here.

Giving a boost to your kids

✓ Send a certificate home each week (make one on the computer) for something your child has done well - being polite, sharing toys, helping Mum etc.

✓ Ask your canteen to supply some 'good work' stickers and stick them on letters and notes to your kids.

✓ Always praise them for something specific when you talk to them on the phone.

✓ Tell them you love them at every opportunity.

✓ Tell them how proud you are of them in front of friends and family.

✓ Listen to them and value their opinion.

For personal study

- Which of the following phrases best describes how good you feel about yourself?
  - I feel worthless
  - I don't feel that good about myself
  - I'm ok about myself
  - I'm very happy with myself

- What phrase would your partner choose to describe how she feels about herself?

- What phrase would your children choose to describe how they feel about themselves?

- Write down three things that you could do to help improve your self-esteem.

- Do the same for your partner and your children.

Chapter 7
Tuning In -
The Importance of Listening

When you've been on a course, have you ever done the exercise where you get into pairs and one of you has to talk for a minute on any subject you want, while the other has to ignore you? Sounds harmless, doesn't it, but the results are quite amazing. A couple of inmates have almost come to blows doing this because one of them got so frustrated with being totally disregarded when he was speaking. If you haven't done this exercise then try it because it really brings home to you how our kids feel when we don't listen to them.

We know it's easy not to listen to our children because we have so many "more important" distractions and they often don't know when to stop talking. Just think of a three-year-old going through their 'Why … ?' stage. The thing is, though, that if we ignore our children when they're young, the chances are that they'll ignore us when they get older.

Listening on visits

Listening to the kids can be difficult on a visit, especially if you've got a number of children there who all want to tell you things at the same time. Maybe you've just had some bad news from the Unit Manager or there's something else that you need to discuss with your partner, but your kids keep interrupting to tell you unimportant things like scoring a goal for the football team or getting all their spellings right in a test. Well, it may be unimportant to you, but it's *very* important to them. If you don't let them tell you all their news straightaway - and remember they will have spent the whole journey bursting to tell you - then they may feel excluded and upset and think that you don't care.

A good idea is to let them talk one at a time. Perhaps sit one child on your knee and cuddle him, while you listen to and look at the other one. Don't be afraid to tell one child to, 'Hang on, I'll hear all your news in a minute,' while you listen to another. Save telling your partner your own news for when the children have gone off to the play area or the shop. By anticipating how to handle these problems beforehand you can prevent any child going home feeling that, 'Dad, hasn't got time for me.'

Of course, some of us can have the opposite problem. What do you do on a visit when your child won't talk to you?

This may be his or her way of dealing with your imprisonment. They may be punishing you for being away from them, or they may simply not be able to cope with the emotions they are going through. Hard though it is, you must accept the situation and not get angry or keep firing questions at them. Let them deal with things in their own time. Try to keep things light-hearted, and try to keep in eye or touch contact with them. A reassuring pat on the shoulder may be the only meaningful contact you have on that visit, but accept it. At least they came to see you and they can see you're OK. Perhaps the next visit will be better.

Listening on the phone

The only other time we are able to listen to our kids is on the phone and this can be a real nightmare. What happens, for instance, when they refuse to come on the line or your credits run out? But although the phone can be a very frustrating tool, at least it's a way of letting the kids hear your voice and having a chat to them. If your finances will run to it, it may be possible to do this on a daily basis.

And if your children don't want to talk? Give them time - you've got plenty of it! With a bit of love and a lot of patience they will eventually come round!

Charlie - 2 years

It's hard to listen on a visit when they all want to talk to you at once, but when the first five minutes is over, they settle down and you get to spend time with them individually.

Damien - 12 months

My teenagers are a nightmare! They spend all the visit acting like they don't want to be there. They won't listen to me one bit!

Paul - 5 years

I'm really proud of my teenage sons. I know they respect and listen to me as I've always listened to their opinions even when they were small.

Listening tips

✓ **Eyeball to eyeball listening**

Some people reckon that you listen more with your eyes
than your ears, so make sure you look your child in the
eye when he particularly needs to know that you are
paying attention. Get down on to his level or sit him on
your knee to make it easier.

✓ **Touchy feely**

Sometimes an affectionate cuddle or a pat on the arm can
tell a child that you really care and that you are
concerned about what they have just told you.

✓ **Repeating what they've said**

If it's not possible to give your child your total attention,
you can still show them that you are listening even though
you're not looking, by repeating their phrase or question
back to them - "You learnt all about stick insects today,
did you?"

✓ **Keeping mum and doing nowt**

Listening may involve saying nothing. Sometimes older
children won't want you to make comments or give advice -

tempting though that might be! Perhaps they just need to get something off their chest - 'I'm finding it really hard at school'. And when this happens you've got to decide not to take over the lead and jump in with comments like, 'Right, I'm ringing up your teacher and sorting it out tomorrow'. Remarks like this are a sure way of making your child keep things to himself.

✓ Listening involves explaining

If we ask our child for her opinion about an important decision and then do the very opposite, she may well think we are ignoring her. Similarly, she may ask things of us that she thinks we just disregard. In these situations, give her the reason why: 'I know you really wanted to go away for your holiday, but we can't afford to. Perhaps if we save hard we can go another time,' or 'I know you wanted to stay with grandma this weekend, but she's poorly. We'll arrange another time as soon as she's better.'

✓ It's OK for them to feel cross

Another important part of listening is to allow our children to express their feelings. Try to encourage them to talk about it: 'I think you must feel very hurt with your friends for leaving you out,' or 'You're angry with me because I won't let you go to the pictures again this week'. Far better than them hitting out at a brother or sister because they are angry!

 # For personal study

- Think about a time in your life when you were not listened to. How did it feel?

- Can you remember a time when you didn't listen to one of your children and they were seriously upset by it? If so, write and apologise to them.

- Make a real effort to listen to each of your children on the next visit.

- Which ways of listening, in the 'Listening Tips' do you find easiest and hardest?

Chapter 8
School Issues -
Helping Your Child Through

The fact is that while we are in prison, school can be a difficult place for our children.

If you live in a small community where everyone knows everyone else's business, then news of your crime will become local gossip and, of course, local children are likely to hear about it through their parents. Perhaps your neighbours will tell their children not to play with your kids anymore. Crimes can become exaggerated and other kids or their parents may spread malicious rumours that will make it difficult for your child to go to school or other social events. It may be that he or she stops being invited to parties any more - this can be devastating for children.

On the other hand, if you live in a big city then it's possible that no-one will know about your sentence. The decision you have to make then is whether or not to tell your child's teacher about your imprisonment.

Do we tell the school?

If you do decide to inform the school it can help the teacher understand why a usually happy and placid child is suddenly displaying symptoms of depression or unhappiness, or that a child's unexplained absences were because they were visiting you in prison. An important advantage is that the teacher can keep a quiet look out for signs of problems such as bullying.

With teenage children who are taking exams it's also worth remembering that teachers can make allowances for a child working under strain at home and, since many exams work on continuous assessment, it is important that a prisoner's child doesn't suffer unduly.

Most inmates, however, confess to not telling the school because they believe the teacher would pick on the child, involve Social Services or make matters worse in some way.

We can't get away from the fact that there's a lot of stigma attached to those who have a criminal record, but much work has been done of late to try and make teachers aware of the special needs of prisoners' children[1]. On the other hand, if you live in an area where quite a few dads (and mums) are in prison then possibly stigma isn't an issue. The school will be aware of the problems associated with imprisonment, and the kids (depending on their parent's crime) may well be treated as heroes!

1. Save the Children has developed an excellent resource, "Working with Children of Prisoners" (June 1998).

Wayne - 4 years

My kid's life at school was hell because of the publicity
about my offence. My wife moved out of the area so he
could change to a new school, but I couldn't believe it
when some spiteful parents spread some rumours there
too. We're having to move for a third time now!

Philip - 3 years

My daughter isn't ashamed that I'm in prison, in fact I got a
Valentine card signed from the entire class!

Stefan - 6 years

My child has suffered a great trauma with me being in
prison. He hasn't been to school for eighteen months. He
just can't cope.

Keeping up to date with your child's progress

If you're separated from your partner and have told your
child's teacher that you are in prison, you can write to the
school and ask for a progress report. This will enable you to
keep fully in touch with any problems (or successes) your
child is experiencing and help you to take more of a part in
his or her education.

If you are still with your partner then she will be able to
keep you up to speed with how the children are doing at
school and any special events. On a visit with the children

the prison may allow her to bring in some school-books so you can help with homework. Perhaps getting your kids to read a book to you, or do some drawings on a visit, will reassure them (and you) that you still care about their work and that it is important.

Craig - 12 years

I read to him on visits. He's five. I'm learning computers so I'll be able to help him when I get out.

Thomas - 12 years

I phone and ask about school every day. I try and answer any problems with their homework.

Rupert - 2 months

He's just learning his first proper sentences so I talk to him and help him a lot on the phone.

Josh - 6 years

My kids are seven, eleven and sixteen so we talk a lot
about school when they visit. I write and ask them how
they are doing as well.

Oscar - 2 years

Me and my daughter are doing the same A level course,
so we help each other out. It's drawn us closer having this
in common. Mind you we're also both determined to get a
better grade than the other!

Ian - 5 months

My kid has had to take a lot of stick because of me
being inside. He deals with it by fighting which gets him
into trouble.

Teaching some things is down to us

As parents we have the responsibility of teaching our children morals - teaching them right from wrong. Unfortunately some of us feel that we don't have the right to do this because we ourselves have committed a crime: 'How can I tell my child it's wrong to steal, when I'm in here for thieving?' It does pose some difficult questions. Others of us feel we can use our own situations in a positive way: 'It's wrong to steal. I did the wrong thing and look what's happened to me. I don't want you to end up the same way.'

Our children's sex education and religious education is also down to us as parents but many don't get involved and leave it to the school. Although schools do take this responsibility seriously it's still important that we give our children opportunities to talk frankly and openly about things they are unsure of. It's also important that we do not force *our* beliefs and opinions on them and to recognise that they have a right to hold a different opinion.

Whether or not we think it should be our responsibility, the fact is that our children will look to *us* for guidance and we must be there to give them a lead.

Family learning

Here at the Wolds we do a number of courses designed to help you to support your child's education. Here's a letter from someone who took part in Family Learning:

The course has been a great success for both me and my boys. We have fully enjoyed our time together and Tom has become far more emotionally stronger and understanding towards the family's situation. He's doing extremely well at school and the school have given him special permission to attend the course - they even send work for us to do together! At home his behaviour is what would be normally expected from a young boy.

Carl, on the other hand, is still at the age where he's testing our patience by being both impish and naughty, but nevertheless he shows good signs in his development.

Family Learning has given my wife and me the opportunity to address a number of the issues that were of concern. In addition, we've also learnt a number of parenting skills that we carry out in order to deal with any problems relating to the behaviour of both Tom and Carl.

I would like to take this opportunity to express my gratitude to my wife for travelling and her participation, to Tom's school for their understanding support, and finally, but by no means least, Sandy and Wolds Prison for their encouraging efforts towards both me and my family ...
thank you.

Dave

Supporting your child at school

✓ Watch out for any signs that seem to point to your child being bullied. Typically, these are loss of appetite, missing school, mood swings, bedwetting or behaviour that is out of character. Contact the school if you are concerned and involve other members of your family to support your child.

✓ Ask your partner to bring in your child's school report. If you're not with your partner, ask the school to send you a copy.

✓ Ask for some books to be available in visits so you can hear your children read each time they come. Get into a routine, but don't get carried away - five minutes maximum!

✓ Ask permission for the kids to bring in their homework or school reading books and help them with it if you can. (Don't do this if you've got teenagers, though - it may be too difficult!)

✓ Get a copy of your child's school report and read it together. Praise and encourage them for all the positive comments … ignore the bad ones.

✓ Buy some 'well done' stickers from the canteen and send one home to congratulate and encourage your child when they've achieved something or been especially well-behaved.

✓ Read the book your child is reading and discuss it with them - Harry Potter is great!

✓ Take part in the Family Learning Programme if your prison runs it.

For personal study

- How is your child coping at school?

- Has your being in prison made a difference to his or her progress or behaviour at school?

- Write down a list of everyday activities through which a child can learn.

- Write down some activities you could do on a visit, or send through the post, to help your child with their school work.

Chapter 9
No Place Like Home -
Preparing for Release

It may seem a little strange to be talking about making preparations for your release when you've only just been sentenced! But for prisoners who have families - especially those with children - this is something to think about and plan for right from the beginning.

Things ain't what they used to be ...

If you are doing a short sentence, your children are young, and you are in a prison near your home, it's probable that when you are released you'll be able to slot back into your old life with a minimum amount of fuss for either you or your family. Your children won't have grown-up too much and your partner's life won't have changed a great deal since you went to prison.

Supposing, however, you've been in prison for six or seven years! In this case, when you're released everything will have changed - life will have moved on. Here are a few things to bear in mind.

Children who weren't much more than babies when you went away will now be teenagers with their own

personalities - probably strong-willed, independent and rebellious! Your daughter, who you may still think of as a little girl, will have matured dramatically and may be resentful that you still treat her as a child. Perhaps your son, who was only five when you went to prison, will now have an issue with you about why it happened and why he wasn't told the truth.

Your partner, too, may have changed - perhaps beyond recognition. She will almost certainly be a stronger, much more independent woman with her own routines and her own way of doing things.

If you've worked hard to address your offending behaviour, and have, perhaps, improved your education and job prospects, the changes in you too will be very obvious. You may well be a different person to the one you were before you were in prison. You may have been a heroin addict before, but will now be coming home clean, healthy and athletic, having spent long hours in the gym. You may have spent your schooldays playing truant, but now, coming out of prison, you might have a list of qualifications a mile long, with RSA's, OCR's, GCSE's and 'Social and Life Skills' certificates coming out of your ears. If you entered prison with very few skills, you may now be leaving with a positive outlook and a new trade behind you - maybe even a few ideas for setting up and running a new business!

In comparison, your partner may have had very little moral or educational support during your imprisonment. Most of her time may have been spent looking after the children. A possible problem you may both have to face and try to get over in this situation is that you may now be poles apart in how you think and behave. You could even be resentful of the change, or lack of change, you see in each other.

Those are a few of the changes we think we could expect - and you can probably think of more that would apply to your own family. But don't stop there! Having anticipated some of the changes, now make up your mind to prepare for them, accept them - and positively look forward to them.

OK - so how <u>do</u> you prepare for release?

It's really best to start preparing to go home on the day you are sentenced. Sounds impossible doesn't it? But if you can look forward and work towards it, you'll be in a much better frame of mind. And it's not just for your benefit - you'll be helping your children especially. Just as *you* can gain an enormous amount of strength and joy from your family, *they* will be in much better emotional shape if they know that you are alright and that you are, at least, reasonably happy.

Make sure that you are still a valued and important member of your family even though you are not with them. Try to be aware of everything that is going on at home. Find out what your partner and the kids are planning and dreaming for the future. In turn, share your plans, hopes and fears with them, so that they know that they are a part of your future, too

We've talked about the importance of staying in contact before, but it's worth saying again because the only way to ensure that you and your family don't grow apart, is to maintain a strong bond with them throughout your sentence. We do understand that this is often very difficult for many prisoners, but even though it's hard, keep trying to have as much contact with your family as is humanly possible. Try to arrange visits as often as you can. Write letters, send cards, and budget your wages or private cash, so that you can talk to your family at least once or twice a week.

At the end of your sentence, when the day of your release finally arrives, the fact that you kept your family unit alive and kicking will go a long way in helping you re-integrate back into society.

John - 9 months

I can't do anything while I'm in prison. I'll just have to wait until I get out and hope for the best.

Dudley - 10 years

There's nothing anyone can do to prepare you for all the changes in your family when you get out.

Stu - 5 years

You sort of imagine that the whole world is going to stop when you're in prison and it's a bit of a shock to find out that everyone has carried on and managed without you!

Steve - 4 years

You've got to keep your eye on the ball from day one or you'll never survive.

Alan - 2 years

I was sick of my life and the mess I got my family into, so I decided as soon as I got in here that enough was enough and I began to plan for my getting out and keeping clean. It's all about getting your head around it and its been easier than I thought...

Malcom - 6 years

Even if you're doing a long stretch you've got to plan for the future. Your family deserve a future.

Expectations ... fantasy v reality

We all have expectations about leaving prison but it's important not to fall into the trap that some prisoners are in.

Often people will be excited for months before their release, building up a fantasy picture of the "outside" as a paradise where they will be able to do everything they ever dreamed of. While this *might* be true for some, most will discover that life "on the out" is fairly ordinary and contains a whole new set of problems - getting a job and earning the money to do all those wonderful things, not being the least of them! This often leads to disappointment, disillusionment and, in some cases, depression.

You may have developed the idea that once you are at home, life will be a "bed of roses", only to discover that's not quite how it is ...

- *You've done a parenting course in prison and now think you know how to be a perfect father. But with kids being kids, things may go wrong in your very first confrontation with them. Instead of the instant obedience you were expecting (having followed one of your tutor's theories), your kids just burst into fits of laughter! Disappointed?*

- *Your family have heard all your promises about "staying clean" and "never going back to jail" before. Now they have trouble believing you and you find you are constantly having to try and prove yourself. Disillusioned?*

- *As soon as you are released, your partner tells you that, having held the fort for so long on her own, she feels it's now your turn to take over the responsibilities of running the home and looking after and disciplining the children. Depressed?*

… Don't expect to succeed at everything, but don't expect to fail. If your expectations are too high, happiness will be hard to find. If your expectations are too low, you may find that your motivation is stunted and that you don't attempt to achieve anything at all. Try to find a balance between the two because, as with most things, the trick with "expectations" is to keep them sensible and, more importantly, keep them realistic.

Jon - 6 months

Everyone was nice to me for the day then it was bang … back to normal.

Callum - 12 months

I'm worried about what my mum's friends will think of me. I'm worried she'll lose her friends because of me.

Kim - 4 years

You feel a bit of an outsider because you've missed so much.

Gareth - 4 years

There's a lot of stigma inside and outside of prison attached to being a criminal.

Phil - 2 months

I didn't know the date I was going to be released and so I didn't know if anyone was going to be there to pick me up.

Don - 18 months

I was really worried about getting out and going back to the situation that put me in prison. I really wished I had somewhere else to go.

Barney - 8 months

I was concerned about other people's views of me.
They thought I might have become a hardened criminal …
people treated me differently.

Jim - 6 years

People don't know how to treat you when you're released
and they're often very wary of you … why can't they
accept that I'm still me?

Max - 8 years

I'm excited and terrified of going back to the family. What if
we can't make a go of it?

We're all creatures of habit, and it's amazing how most families are held together by routine. It's well known, for example, that a lot of couples fight and argue for the first few days of a holiday, until their new roles and routines are sorted out.

So here we have a new situation - you've just been released from prison and are really excited to be back in the bosom of your family where everything will be "just like it used to be". Think again!! *Nothing* is "like it used to be", things are not done the same way anymore, your family's routines have changed completely.

Although you may feel awkward at first, a bit powerless or a bit like a "spare part", a wise man will take his time and slowly ease his way into the new routines. Try not to disturb and upset the smooth running of the family and the household, but instead, become a part of it.

It's the same with the issue of discipline. Do you come in and take over where you left off? The answer has to be a resounding NO! But neither should you do nothing, as this will only leave you feeling useless at leaving your partner to handle it on her own as before. A good idea is to talk discipline issues through with your partner, back up her decisions and take a positive, but gentle attitude.

Remember that your family has had a life without you. They may now have new hobbies, careers and friends. You must encourage all this to continue without feeling sorry for yourself, left out or resentful. Instead, take an interest in what they are doing and look for new hobbies and interests yourself, getting your family involved where you can.

We believe the key thing during your stay in prison is to keep in touch with your family as much as you possibly can. And when you are released, take things slowly and aim to fit in around them. Always remember though, you are still "Dad", and you can, and should, play a major part in the life of your family. Go for it!

 **For personal study**

- Are you thinking about and preparing for release?

- Write down your children's ages and what stages they were at when you first came into prison - for example, she may have been a year old and just learning to walk. Research the stages they will be at when you are released - for example, if they will be teenagers, find out all you can about typical teenage behaviour!

- Make a list of things you could do to prepare yourself for the changes you will find.

Chapter 10
So Can You Really Be a Good
Dad in Prison?

Let's hear it from the lads ...

Gazza - 6 years

Yes, of course you can be a good dad. I set some guidelines early on for the eldest to accept and for the younger ones to follow on.

Lee - 4 years

Yes, you can be a good dad, but you have to really want to carry on.

Miles - 7 years

I'm not as good a dad as I want to be, but you can't give up!

Matthew - 6 months

I know I'm not there, but I still try and encourage my values.

Chris - 10 years

In my opinion the key to being an effective 'prison father' is without doubt communication. What is important is not just the quantity - how many visits or how many phone-calls you can have - but the quality. I find you must be prepared to listen to what they say no matter how trivial it may seem to you, it's obviously important to your child or they would not be talking about it. Prison life has nothing to do with your family, just take what joy you can in your children and enjoy being with them for the short time you are with them.

Mark - 12 months

I feel like I've let my kids down but I'm doing my best to become a better dad and person while I'm in prison. Fingers crossed!

Liam - 2 years

I thought I was a good father. It's only after coming to prison I've realised I didn't have a clue and that I tried to buy the affection of my children. I now know that anyone can be a dad, but not everyone can be a father. I've lost so much precious time finding excuses not to be with my family, they don't stay kids for long. I'm due to be released soon and I'm going back to be a proper father now.

Wayne - 8 years

Just because we're not there in body does not mean we have to give up. Always remember we can love from a distance. I have met many prisoners who feel that they should give up and go to sleep and never wake up, but when you start to think about your children there is always a good memory to look back on and things do not look as black. Keep on hoping.

It sounds corny, but some dads come to prison and learn how to be better dads than they were before!

> Well, Sandy, what can I say but, thanks to you, my kids are so good with me. My son, Jamie, well, he won't let me out of his sight and I think it's all down to you. Because of Family Learning I have so much time for my kids now, I don't think of myself just sat down doing nothing, I go out with them and we all have so much fun. The pub can wait.
>
> **Steve**

It's easy to become discouraged and feel you're a failure as a dad when you're in prison but the *amount* of time we can spend with our kids isn't the be all and end all.

There are men out there 24/7 who still don't spend time with their children. A survey of a group of dads asked them, 'How long do you think you spend each day in conversation with your toddlers?' Most of the men guessed at between fifteen and twenty minutes a day and, to test this, the researchers put microphones on them to measure it accurately. The researchers found that on average the men talked for less than forty seconds a day with their children! … So dads in prison aren't alone in the short amount of time they have with their kids.

Loving them against the odds

The real issue for us here is not *how much time* you spend with your kids, but the *quality of love* you give them. And it's not just about when we're with them during visits, it's about *all* our contact - including phone calls and letters.

Of course we can't pretend that your kids won't be disappointed that you aren't there for things like the school play or the football match, but if you ask them to send you things about the event (such as photos, or the programme with their name in) then you'll be showing them that you care and would have been there if you could. For the children, it will be nearly as good as having you there and it will help them explain to their friends that although Dad couldn't come, he really wanted to.

Compare this to a father on the out who forgets to turn up, or doesn't even ask about how the event went. We know which kind of dad we would want to have ... and we know which kind of dad we want be!

And finally ...

Go for it! You *can* be a good dad while you're in prison. We can't pretend it's easy, sometimes far from it, but it's well worth all the effort - you'll never regret it!

Hope this helps ... we wish you all the best!

For personal study

- Which of the following would descibe how good a dad you feel you can be in prison:
  - Bad
  - Not very good
  - Good
  - Very good

- Write a list of the roles you can still carry out as a dad while you are in prison.

- Write out a list of the roles you feel you cannot do while in prison.

- Does the age of your child make a difference as to whether or not you can fulfil these roles?

Group Discussion Questions

Social and Life Skills Tutors' Guide

Appendix -
Useful Organisations

Group Discussion Questions

This section of the book is designed as an aid for discussion/study group leaders who are helping their groups develop the topics covered in "Daddy's Working Away".

Chapter 1
Going to Jail

1 Discuss the issues that are raised in Sally's story.

2 How can the public be educated about what life is like in prison?

3 Discuss Chloe's problem with her child. What could you do to help a child cope when her father is put in prison?

Chapter 2
The Big Question - What Do We Tell the Kids?

1 Discuss the pro's and con's of telling your child that, 'Daddy's working away'.

2 Discuss the problems involved when you want to tell your child the truth, but your partner or parents have told them you are working away.

3 Vince said, 'I've told her that I'm in prison for being naughty'. How much can you tell your child about your offence?

Chapter 3
It's Good to Talk - Keeping in Contact

1 Discuss the suggestion that, 'It's better all round to cut family ties and do our time hard core.'

2 Do you agree with the idea that visits have to be planned - for example, writing down questions and jokes to use?

3 What are the issues that arise when you want to have contact with your children but are no longer with your partner?

Chapter 4
Wait 'til Your Father Gets Home! - Discipline

1 Your child misbehaves on a visit. Discuss what the problems are if you tell him off, and the problems that may result if you do not tell him off!

2 It has been suggested that you should balance every one negative thing you say to your child by four positive things. How good are you at praising and encouraging your child?

3 What could you do if your partner had a very different way of dealing with the kids than you - for example, she believed in smacking and you did not?

Chapter 5
Money, Money, Money

1 'It's a man's job to provide for his family.' Discuss.

2 In what ways might a prison sentence affect a family's finances?

3 Discuss possible ways of surviving on a limited budget when you have children.

Chapter 6
Because You're Worth It! - You and Your Family

1 'Having low self-esteem is like driving with the handbrake on'. Discuss.

2 Do you agree with the part in the book that says prison provides lots of opportunities for men to build their self-esteem?

3 Do you think that Listeners play an important role in the prison?

Chapter 7
Tuning In - The Importance of Listening

1 'Listening has more to do with our eyes than our ears.' Discuss.

2 Paul, who is doing five years, says, 'I'm really proud of my
   teenage sons. I know they respect and listen to me as I've
   always listened to their opinions, even when they were small.'
   Comment on the possible reasons why Paul seems to have a
   good relationship with his teenagers. Compare Paul's quote
   with Damian's.

3 What do you think it means when the book suggests, 'listening
   involves action'?

Chapter 8
School Issues - Helping Your Child Through

1 'As parents we have the responsibility of teaching our children
   morals; teaching them right from wrong.' Discuss.

2 Talk about the problems of bullying that a child may face at
   school. Suggest ways to help the child cope.

3 Suggest how a dad can keep up with his child's progress at
   school if he is separated from his partner.

Chapter 9
No Place Like Home - Preparing for Release

1 'Making preparations for your release must start on the day you are sentenced.' Discuss.

2 What adjustments might you need to make to allow for changes in your partner?

3 'Don't expect to succeed at everything, but don't expect to fail'. How can you maintain a balanced view of the future?

Chapter 10
So Can You Really Be a Good Dad in Prison?

1 What do you make of the results of the survey that found that some dads, who thought they spent 15-20 minutes per day in conversation with their toddlers, actually spent less than 40 seconds talking with them?

2 Geoff says, 'In my opinion the key to being an effective prison father is, without a doubt, communication'. How can communication be improved between a prisoner and his family?

3 'Being in prison has done me the world of good'. Rehabilitation or rhetoric?

Social and Life Skills Tutors' Guide

The section has been written for tutors of the Social and Life Skills course. Each chapter of the book is mapped to some aspect of the Parentcraft Module but tutors should use supplementary material in order to achieve the full assessment criteria.

Chapter 1
Going to Jail

Entry Assessment Criteria 2.1:
       Identify the individual basic rights of children within the family unit.

       Assessment Criteria 7.1:
       Identify his own needs as a parent.

       Assessment Criteria 7.2:
       Suggest how these needs can be met.

Level 1 Assessment Criteria 2:
        Identify the individual basic rights and needs of parents, children and other members of the family.

Level 2   Assessment Criteria 2:
           Identify the individual rights and needs of parents,
           children and different members within the family.
           Suggest ways in which these can be met as children
           grow and develop.

Chapter 2
The Big Question - What Do We Tell the Kids?

Level 1   Assessment Criteria 3:
           Give examples of the importance of being honest
           with children.

Level 2   Assessment Criteria 3:
           Give examples of the importance of being honest
           with children at different stages in their development.

Chapter 3
It's Good to Talk - Keeping in Contact

Entry   Assessment Criteria 2.1:
           Identify the individual basic rights of children within the
           family unit.

           Assessment Criteria 7.1:
           Identify his own needs as a parent.

           Assessment Criteria 7.2:
           Suggest how these needs can be met.

Level 1   Assessment Criteria 2:
Identify the individual basic rights and needs of parents, children and other members of the family.

Level 2   Assessment Criteria 2:
Identify the individual basic rights and needs of parents, children and different members of the family and suggest ways in which these can be met as children grow and develop.

Chapter 4
Wait 'til Your Father Gets Home! - Discipline

Entry   Assessment Criteria 4.1:
For children of different ages, state at least one example of 'difficult' behaviour.

Assessment Criteria 5.1:
Suggest one way in which a parent could deal with 'difficult' behaviour in the examples given above.

Level 1   Assessment Criteria 5a:
Identify and outline basic techniques and strategies that might be used to cope with children's behaviour in given situations.

Level 2   Assessment Criteria 5a:
Outline techniques and strategies that might be used to cope with children's behaviour in given situations. Identify advice and support agencies that are available.

Chapter 5
Money, Money, Money

Entry   Assessment Criteria 1.1:
          List the main roles of the parent in the family unit.

Level 1   Assessment Criteria 1:
          Identify the major responsibilities of parenthood.

Level 2   Assessment Criteria 1:
          Discuss their responsibilities as a parent and identify how
          these may change in the future.

Chapter 6
Because You're Worth It! - You and Your Family

Entry   Assessment Criteria 1.1:
          List the main roles of the parent in the family unit.

Level 1   Assessment Criteria 1:
          Identify the major responsibilities of parenthood.

Level 2   Assessment Criteria 1:
          Discuss their responsibilities as a parent and identify
          how these may change in the future.

Chapter 7
Tuning In - The Importance of Listening

Entry   Assessment Criteria 3.1:
           Give examples of situations in which it is important to listen to children.

Level 1   Assessment Criteria 4:
           Give examples of situations in which it is important to listen to children and offer choices back.

Level 2   Assessment Criteria 4:
           Give examples of situations in which it is important to listen to children and suggest ways to offer choices at different stages in their development.

Chapter 8
School Issues - Helping Your Child Through

Entry   Assessment Criteria 6.1:
           Identify everyday family activities in which children learn.

           Assessment Criteria 6.2:
           Suggest a practical activity parents and children could do together to help the children learn.

Level 1   Assessment Criteria 6:
           Identify ways in which children learn through daily activities and suggest ways in which parents can develop this.

Level 2   Assessment Criteria 6:
           Explain ways in which children learn through daily
           activities and suggest practical ways in which parents can
           develop this.

Chapter 9
No Place Like Home - Preparing for Release

Entry   Assessment Criteria 2.1:
           Identify the individual basic rights of children within the
           family unit.

           Assessment Criteria 7.1:
           Identify his own needs as a parent.

           Assessment Criteria 7.2:
           Suggest how these needs can be met.

Level 1   Assessment Criteria 2:
           Identify the individual basic rights and needs of parents,
           children and other members of the family.

           Assessment Criteria 7:
           Identify their own needs and suggest a plan of action for
           beginning to meet these.

Level 2   Assessment Criteria 2:
           Identify the individual rights and needs of parents and
           children and different members within the family and
           suggest ways in which these can be met as children
           grow and develop.

Chapter 10
So Can You Really Be a Good Dad in Prison?

Entry   Assessment Criteria 1.1:
         List the main roles of the parent in the family unit.

Level 1   Assessment Criteria 1:
         Identify the major responsibilities of parenthood.

Level 2   Assessment Criteria 2:
         Discuss their responsibilities as a parent and identify how
         these may change in the future.

Appendix - Useful Organisations

Action for Prisoners' Families
Riverbank House
1 Putney Bridge Approach
London
SW6 3JD
Tel: 020 7384 1987
Helpline: 0808 808 2222
Website: www.prisonersfamilies.org.uk
National federation of charities in England and Wales supporting families of prisoners.

ADFAM
Waterbridge House
32-36 Loman Street
London
SE1 0EH
Tel: 020 7928 8898
Website: www.adfam.org.uk
National charity for families with drugs and alcohol problems.

Alcoholics Anonymous (AA)
Tel: 0845 769 7555
Website: www.alcoholics-anonymous.org.uk
Help and advice for people who have a drink problem.

Assisted Prison Visits Unit (APVU)

PO Box 2152
Edgbaston
Birmingham
B15 1SD
Helpline: 0845 300 1423
Offers help for people on a low income with travelling expenses to visit close relatives in prison.

Childline

Helpline: 0800 11 11
Free national helpline for children and young people in the UK.

National Association of Citizens' Advice Bureau

Tel: See phone directory for local branch.
Web: www.nacb.org.uk
Local bureaux and website offering advice, information or advocacy on a wide range of issues.

National Association for the Care and Resettlement of Offenders (NACRO)

169 Clapham Road
London
SW9 010
Tel: 020 7582 6500
Website: www.nacro.org.uk
National charity in England and Wales giving ex-offenders help to build a better future.

National Drugs Helpline

Helpline: 0800 77 66 00

Free 24-hour helpline offering advice and information for those with concerns about drugs and solvents.

Parentline Plus

Helpline: 0800 800 222

Website: www:parentlineplus.org.uk

Free helpline offering telephone support to any parent or carer of children finding it difficult to cope.

Prison Fellowship England and Wales

Prison Fellowship

PO Box 945

Maldon

Essex

CM9 4EW

Tel: 01621 843232

Website: www.prisonfellowship.org.uk

Providing ongoing support to prisoners, ex-prisoners and their families.

Care for the Family

Care for the Family is a national charity committed to strengthening family life and helping those who are hurting because of family breakdown.

Since it was founded in 1988, over two hundred thousand people have attended seminars on marriage, parenting and other family issues.

International speaker, Rob Parsons is the organisation's Executive Director and is also the best-selling author of 'The Sixty Minute Father' and 'The Heart of Success'.

For further details, please write to Care for the Family, PO Box 488, Cardiff CF15 7YY, telephone (029) 2081 0800 or visit us online at www.care-for-the-family.org.uk